LIFE IN THE SPIRIT

By
Jessie Penn-Lewis

CHRISTIAN • LITERATURE • CRUSADE
Fort Washington, Pennsylvania 19034

CHRISTIAN LITERATURE CRUSADE

U.S.A.
Box 1449, Fort Washington, PA 19034

GREAT BRITAIN
51 The Dean, Alresford, Hants. SO24 9BJ

NEW ZEALAND
P.O. Box 77, Ashurst

Originally published by

THE OVERCOMER LITERATURE TRUST
England

First American edition
Revised 1991
This Printing 1995

ISBN 0-87508-956-9

Scripture quotations from:
The King James Version unless otherwise indicated.
The American Standard Version (*ASV*), 1901,
    Thomas Nelson & Sons, New York.
The Epistles of Paul (a translation and notes) by
    W. J. Conybeare, England (died 1857).
The New Testament in Modern Speech,
    R. F. Weymouth, 1903, 1924, England.

Printed in Colombia

IMPRESO EN COLOMBIA
BUENA SEMILLA
Apartado 29724
Bogotá, Colombia

CONTENTS

1. The Heavenly Warfare 7

2. The Warfare and the Weapons 21

3. A Glimpse into Life in the Spirit 39

4. The Revelation of the Victor 55

5. Overcoming the Accuser 69

6. Believe Not Every Spirit 77

CHAPTER 1

THE HEAVENLY WARFARE

"Your adversary the devil . . . whom withstand stedfast in the faith" (1 Peter 5:8–9, ASV).

WITH the purpose of learning something about spirit-warfare we will turn to the sixth chapter in Ephesians, and in so doing we will listen to Paul, who wrote this letter from a prison. Though he was in a Roman prison, his spirit was in triumph with Christ, in the place of victory, and Paul in Rome and in prison is ministering to the church today. Looking at him from the outside, one might be tempted to say: "Poor Paul, his work is ended." "No, no," he would answer, "there is no defeat in the heavenly places." This is the man who wrote of the highest things that concern the spiritual life of the church; and this revelation we have in this wonderful Epistle to the Ephesians.

It begins with the revelation of Christ seated at God's right hand, and closes with the message of the Christian's conflict in the sixth chapter. Let us look at it, sentence by sentence.

In the tenth verse of chapter six it says, "Finally"; in the margin [of the 1881 Revised Version] it is, "From henceforth." Let us read it as from August 1st in this Llandrindod Convention tent—"From henceforth be strong." Be strong in what? In a spiritual position, "IN THE LORD." You are in Him. Where He is, you are. You are joined to Him in spirit. Do you know it? Well, *live* there! "Be strong in the Lord." Not in your own opinions, not in your own strength, but "be strong" in a person—and that person the Lord. Have only Christ as your center, and as your life, and as your strength, and as your power. It is the Lord, *the Lord*, "The LORD strong and mighty, the LORD mighty in battle." Not in yourself, not in your circumstances, not in your place, not in your plans—be strong in nothing else but "in the Lord"!

We need to pause here and go over the steps of the believer's path into the position of victory. To be strong in the Lord for the spirit-warfare of Ephesians 6, we must first be "in the Lord" in His *death*. "Know ye not, that so many of us as were baptized *into Jesus Christ*, were baptized into His death?" (Romans 6:3). You must be planted in His death (v. 5) before you can be strong in His life. He does not say that He is going to make your life strong. He does not say that He is going to make *you* anything! You are to be planted, to be rooted, to be deep down in His death, so that nothing can tear you out—so that not all the forces of hell can draw you out of your deep-rooted place in His death; "baptized," "planted *into His death*," so that you may be so united in spirit to Him as to "be strong" in *His* life. "Reckon ye also yourselves to be dead indeed unto sin, but alive unto God through Jesus Christ" (Romans 6:11). Then "Be strong in His life, as the ascended One." That is the position for your spirit—not for your body, not for your soul. "He that is joined unto the Lord is one *spirit*" (1 Corinthians 6:17). Not a mixture of soul and spirit, but the "soul" poured out unto death—as we are planted into His death so that the spirit is liberated and joined to Him who is the Overcomer seated above principalities and powers in the heavenlies.

"And in the *strength of His might*": To "be strong in the Lord" means to be strong in the strength of His might. According to the first chapter of Ephesians, the "strength of His might" (v. 19, *ASV*) is the very strength that lifted Christ from the dead, and set Him at God's right hand. That very strength of His might can enter into your spirit, and lift it to

the place of victory. Your spirit will never *get*
there but as it is actually joined to the One
who *is* there. "In the strength of *His might*":
that very same strength that lifted the dead
Christ from His tomb and took Him right
through the "powers of the air," for He passed
through them into the heavens, and sat down.
Be strong in that position of the spirit, even
that Spirit-strength which comes from union
with Him who overcame and sat down in the
place of victory and power.

We are so anxious about our bodies. We
want our bodies strong; but if your spirit is
strong, your body will become strengthened.
Your body is not to carry your spirit, but your
spirit should control your body. For this the
spirit must be made strong by the strength of
His might, and this is given by spirit-food. The
Word of God is spirit-food. The words He has
spoken to us, they are "spirit and life." When
your spirit is strong, it assimilates the spirit-
food in the Bible, and you feed your spirit.
You need a strong spirit more than a strong
body, and even more than a strong mind.
Your mind, however, will be stronger if you
have a strong spirit to quicken it, for in that
spirit dwells the Holy Spirit. It is the shrine of
God. It is the place where God dwells, and the
strength of the might of God is to get into your
spirit until your spirit is "strong in the Lord,
and in the strength of His might" (*ASV*).

Have you asked God to make your *spirit*
strong (Luke 1:80), and do you use the means

provided for making it strong? How? By not only feeding it, but exercising it. A strong spirit comes by exercise. This is why God permits conflict. *Your spirit grows strong in conflict*, and that is why God permits the warfare.

Notice the way in which the spirit gets strong in the Lord. It is given in the eleventh verse of this chapter: "Put on the whole armour of God, *that ye may be able to stand* against the wiles of the devil." Does it say "against the wiles of the world"? No. Of the people? No, but "*of the devil.*" Here we see a spirit-position given to stand upon against an unseen spirit-foe exercising "wiles" for some specific purpose. They are to draw you down from your position. If I went through this tent and inquired, I should probably find that many of God's children have been drawn down. You once knew the song of victory—how to shout the shout of victory, and see the Lord disperse the foe; but the "wiles" have worked around you, and the shout has gone. They have brought to you dark clouds, exaggerated to you all kinds of things, placed pictures in your mind, planned all sorts of things to draw you down. Did you put on the whole armor of God, to stand in your spirit-position "in the Lord" against the wiles of the devil?

Read what comes next: "*For* our wrestling is not against flesh and blood" (v. 12, *ASV*). This conflict is not in the realm of earth, and you are not to walk in that realm. The wrestling is with the enemy at the *back* of the "flesh and blood" (see Ephesians 2:2). Believe me, children of God, if you would learn to attack the foe at the back, claiming the victory in the name of the Lord Jesus, nothing could stand before you, nor before the shout of victory in Christ's name.

"We wrestle against." It is a wrestling. It means standing *in spirit* against something that is coming against you *in spirit.* When you really know spiritual union with Christ, you will be distinctly conscious of the approach of this unseen foe coming against you. Since the Holy Spirit is dwelling in your spirit, there will come in your spirit instantly a sharp resistance springing spontaneously "against" the unseen foe, and your vision will get more acute to detect this. For instance, in practical life, you may meet with someone who will tell you a dark story. Instead of taking the story, you will see the foul enemy behind it; and you will say, "No, I won't take that." That is one way in which you "stand against" the principalities and powers who are using "flesh and blood." Our wrestling is against these— against the powers, against the world-rulers. The "world-rulers," who are they? Doesn't God rule? God is surely sovereign *on the throne*, but in this dispensation the god of this age is ruling the darkness; and the darkness in yonder valley where you work is the darkness of the world-rulers. You see it, you feel it. Have you understood how to wrestle with these world-rulers, and triumph, so that you hold the victory? . . . and to stand in spirit strong in the Lord and the strength of His might against the foe?

"And against spiritual hosts of wickedness" (*ASV*);or, as it really is—"wickednesses that are spirits." There is the drink wickedness: that is the spirit of drink. The tattling wickedness: that is the spirit of tattling. Perhaps you haven't understood the "wickednesses that are spirits" when these foes were attacking you and pushing you to do things that you did not want to do in your heart. All this is because you did not understand the actual cause of the trouble, and did not know how to stand in the Lord and in the strength of His might, and hold the victory. Here is the spirit-conflict: *"against the principalities and powers, the world-rulers of this darkness, the wickednesses that are spirits"* (*paraphrase*). Then what use is it to argue with men? Deal with the wickedness that is a spirit!

"Wherefore *take up* the whole armor" (*ASV*). Here we see the action of the will. The Lord does not "will" instead of you. He will do everything for you—yes—but you have to exercise your right of choice. He will give you the power, but you must choose. "That ye may be able to stand" (v. 11). Here is an onslaught of the enemy. There is a "standing against," and in addition to that there is an onslaught which the apostle describes as an "evil day." "That ye may be able to stand in the *'evil day'"* (see v.

13). There is an evil day, and there are days that are evil. You rise in the morning sometimes and you say, "This is an evil day"; and so you find it. What will you do? Take the armor, and say, "Lord, I understand that there is an onslaught today. I am conscious of the approach of the enemy. The devil has a scheme today; he is working out a plan—there are the indications of it. Now, Lord, I *take* by faith the whole armor, that I may be able to stand in this evil day."

Now, notice in regard to the armor that in verse 14 there are mentioned three distinct sections of the Christian's armor, under the names of "truth," "righteousness," and "steadfastness." The very *first* preparation for this battle is having your mind filled with truth. Paul says, "*Gird up your loins with truth*," while Peter explains that it is the loins of the *mind* that are to be so girded: "*Gird up the loins of the mind*" (1 Peter 1:13). You must fill your mind with truth. You must be willing to have nothing but the truth. No theory or theories—they will all get broken in this warfare. It is the mind you must gird first. If your mind is filled with novels, you will not have any victory; and if your mind is filled with your own thoughts, it is very poor stuff with which to stand against the enemy. If, however, your mind is filled with *truth*, then, when the enemy attacks you, you have an answer for him in the word of Scripture; and that, too, in a moment, for the sudden attacks of the enemy often give you no time to fetch the Book.

Do you know how to fight using the Word of God, and what to do when the onslaught comes in your private life? Do you know, when heavy oppression comes on your spirit, how to break through it all in spirit by using the truth of God? Do you understand how to wield the victory texts, such as: "The Son of God was manifested that He might destroy the works of the devil"; "that through death He might destroy him that had the power of death, that is, the devil"; "they overcame him by the blood of the Lamb, and by the word of their testimony, and they loved not their lives even unto death"? Begin, then, with your texts, and use them until your spirit is free and rejoicing in victory, and you see the conquest of Christ over the foe.

You have been under depression, and thought it physical! You thought you were "very tired"; you said that you had "no message"! You became dumb—when you met needy souls you had nothing to say to them! You thought that you must have grieved the Lord. Someone came to you in trouble, and you could not impart any comfort! Or others came with gossip, and you had no power to resist it, and to sweep away by a word of light and power the tattling spirits which you saw. Then, too, there are the private meetings of the Lord's children when they pass on from one to the other the spirit of depression, which they do not recognize and immediately refuse because they do not discern the working of the "power of the air" at work around them!

If you are physically tired, that is no reason why your *spirit* should be crushed. You are on the *winning side* with the victorious Christ and can afford to wait! You who know the Living Lord, rise and take your place in spirit "in the Lord," and throw off this cloud that is on you. There is a cloud of pessimism and depression on Wales just now. There is power locked up in God's faithful children enough to shake the land again, if that power could only break through the weight which has come upon it. Were not most of us ignorant when the supernatural forces fell upon our land? Were we not as those who were walking in a strange realm, knowing little what was happening? We did not understand clearly about the principalities and powers, and, in our ignorance, all these dark hosts gathered around and slowly stole again upon the land that God had claimed. They stole upon the church, and even upon the living witnesses of revival, and bore upon them the crushing weight of opposition and darkness, criticism, unkindness and coldness.

Much has been learned since then, but have we yet understood how to throw off the cloud of the enemy and in spirit keep moving on in victory? Then you can live in the darkest place and still live in the light of the Sun of Righteousness. There is *a sphere above the sphere of darkness*, and that is your right place! Pember says that the expression "the power of the air" refers to "thick and misty air"—showing that the realm around our planet consists of "thick and misty air" under the control of the prince of the power of the air. Above that is the sunlight, where the ascended Son of God sits waiting for His enemies to be made the footstool of His feet. When you pray "Oh, that Thou wouldst rend the heavens and come down," you are asking God to break through the thick and misty air, and by prayer you are making way for Him. He wants a link below. He can rend the heavens, He can rend this thick, misty air in answer to our prayers, and come down in melting power among His people.

When your spirit gets down into a mist you may know you have been drawn down into the lower realm of the enemy But when your spirit is in unbroken communion with Christ, then you will know what He wants you to do! The Holy Spirit dwells in your spirit: if you live in the deep stillness with Him, you will come to detect the slightest movings of that Spirit. When there has been no move in your spirit, and you have acted, then things have gone wrong. What blundering babes we have been! How merciful it has been of God to use us! No wonder the powers of darkness have taken advantage of our ignorance; but God has given us light, that we may become intelligent soldiers for a triumphant warfare.

Just briefly let us look at the only aggressive portion of this passage. The eighteenth verse is the aggressive verse—the climax of the whole, revealing the aggressive weapon of the warrior. *"With all prayer and supplication praying at all seasons in the spirit"* (*paraphrase*). It does not say "on your knees." It does not say "aloud." It does not say "alone"; but it does say *"in the spirit." "All seasons"*; that is to say, ceaseless prayer in your spirit. If you are ceaselessly praying "in the spirit" you keep the enemy at bay. If you are prayerless, you let him in. In this conflict you must always be abiding in victory by prayer. There should always be coming from you a stream of prayer, proceeding from your spirit wherein the Holy Spirit dwells. This is because you are always on the attack. Let the aggressive prayer stream stop, and you will find the enemy will press in upon you.

Think of what this would mean, if you walked everywhere with ceaseless and aggressive prayer. And for whom should you pray? *"For all saints."*

Then the apostle adds, "Praying at all seasons, with all perseverance for all saints, *and for me, that utterance may be given unto me, that I may open my mouth boldly and speak as I ought to speak*" (see vs. 18–20). But Paul, I thought you had had a baptism of the Holy Spirit; you surely do not need prayer for the opening of your mouth boldly! Yes, Paul understood the conflict. No man will preach the gospel in truth and power if the devil can stop him, yet many of you have left your minister in the pulpit without your prayers. You have let the enemy deceive him, and lead him to preach a "gospel" that is *not* a gospel. You have blamed the *man*, and you have not understood that the power which has blinded his eyes and drawn him aside was "in the air." He did not know the power of God enough to enable him to resist the forces in the air, and the devil attacked his mind and put into it all kinds of things that in his heart *he would not say if he knew what he was saying.*

There are men who are wounding the Lord Jesus today who would cut their hands off rather than do it knowingly. There are men who love the Lord Jesus Christ who are saying things that are *not* a gospel from Him, and they do not know it. "And for me, that utterance may be given unto me." If you see a man preaching the real gospel today, you see a man that the devil will attack to the utmost. He will try every trick possible to switch him off the truth. Pray for God's messengers; pray for the men who stand in the pulpit. Pray that they may live in the light of Calvary. Take to prayer . . . but take to the prayer of *victory*, take to the prayer of *mastery*, take to the prayer that *receives* what it asks, take to the prayer that can *bind* the devil, that can *deliver souls*! May God take us into it, and from henceforth let us "be strong in the Lord, and in the strength of His might" (*ASV*), to stand unshaken in this evil day, against the forces of darkness contesting every step of the church's advance to the place of victory in her ascended Lord.

CHAPTER 2

THE WARFARE AND THE WEAPONS

"The weapons of our warfare are not of the flesh, but mighty . . ." (2 Corinthians 10:4, ASV).

WE HAVE understood a little about service, but not much about conflict, especially conflict service. The warfare which we have known is mostly personal temptation, and how to get victory over sin. But with all the light given at our conventions this question of personal victory should now be a settled matter with *those who are in God's service.*

Let us turn again to Ephesians 6, and revolve round its message in these Workers' Meetings. Please put aside what is not clear to you, but commit it to the Holy Spirit to be

brought back to you later on. I remember a
sentence of Pastor Stockmayer's once coming
back to me when at the point of death. I had
power in the spirit to lay hold of it, and it
saved my life. Naturally you wish to *understand*, but it is better that you should not try
to grasp everything with your mind, but qui-
etly let the Lord put it there ready for His use
later on. It will come back to you when you
need it, if you will not dislodge it by discuss-
ing and dissecting it. The seed of the truth
needs to be left to lie in the mind in quiet until
it is quickened by the Spirit of God.

This warfare is not an earthly warfare,
nor is it entirely a warfare of temptation—a
warfare of overcoming some sin. It is the warfare of one who is united with the ascended
Christ, clothed with the luminous garments
of the whole armor of God, for God has provided a luminous garment to clothe His re-
deemed ones through which the "fiery darts of
the wicked one" cannot penetrate; and that
luminous garment is called "the armor of
light." It is "the whole armor of God," the
clothing for the spirit of the believer—for "the
new man in Christ Jesus."

This, I say, is a warfare of the spirit, and
in the spiritual realm. Those who are still
"men of soul"—that is the natural man—do
not understand it. You talk to them, and they
do not know your language. There are two
separate planes altogether: the victorious life
lived on "earthly ground," and the victorious

warfare *in the unseen sphere*—the plane where, united to the Victor and in His victory, we master the unseen forces of the powers of darkness.

The Spirit of God is working in the church to press forward the body of Christ—experientially, I mean, for it is already there judicially—into this "heavenly" sphere, the sphere which Paul knew and lived in. We have known so little about it that we are like strangers in it, knowing no "landmarks" and therefore ignorant often of the way.

We have already dealt with Paul's description of this warfare in the words "for our wrestling is not against flesh and blood" (ASV). It is manifestly not a question of victory over sin. Let me repeat that this question of victory over sin ought to be an absolutely settled matter with every believer through an intelligent understanding of our death with Christ on Calvary. If we rightly apprehend our position, understanding that "our old man" has been crucified with Christ, and reckoning ourselves, hour by hour, "dead indeed unto sin," then we have entered upon this conflict in the spiritual sphere. Now we begin to understand this wrestling in the spirit. Not with your "soul," or with your mind, or with your feeling, or with your emotions, or with your body, but with your *spirit*. It is a spiritual conflict with a spiritual foe, waged with spiritual weapons, with spiritual power.

"Our wrestling is not against flesh and

blood, but against the principalities, against the powers, against the world-rulers of this darkness" (*ASV*). Bear with me while I lift the veil a little, and show you the spiritual forces against which we wrestle.

Let us turn to Genesis 1, and see how we get a hint there of the sphere occupied by the opposing forces of principalities and powers. The only portion of the created world which God did not pronounce "very good" was the firmament or expanse, which He called "sky" or "heavens" (vs. 6–8)—in Hebrew, *shamayim.* In the latter part of the chapter (v. 28) this Hebrew word is translated "air." The Lord Jesus speaks in His parable of the Sower and the Seed about the "fowls of the air," which He explains to be Satan and his forces (Matthew 13:19). And the Epistle to the Hebrews speaks of "things in the heavens" needing cleansing. There is a cleansing of the air which can only be done through the work of Christ at Calvary. The Lord did not say "very good" when He created the expanse, because of these unseen forces there.

Again you have a clear confirmation of this in Ephesians 2:2, where Paul says, "In time past ye walked according to the course of this world, *according to the prince of the power of the air.*" The apostle unequivocally states that "the course of this world" is governed by "the prince of the air"; and the sooner we face that fact the better, as we talk of "the world getting better," and of a golden age of a Christianized heathendom. If we walk according to the course of this world, we are not walking according to God, but "according to"—that is, in accord with—the prince of the air, who governs an opposing monarchy ranged against God and His Son Jesus Christ. The Lord Jesus spoke about Beelzebub as the "prince" of the evil hosts, and in Daniel we have a glimpse of his chief princes, the prince of Persia and the prince of Grecia—mighty angels under his rule, forming a hierarchy of power, the "power of the air"—in united opposition to the Kingdom of Christ, who in the counsel of God is the predestined Lord of the universe.

In the Bible you are shown clearly how Satan works through all these forces. No wonder he is busy making men doubt the inspiration of the Scriptures, and doing all he can to hinder men from reading them—lest they have their eyes opened to his existence and ways. You will discover that the prince of the opposing confederation against God is the one who "walks about." When he came before God about Job he said he came from "walking up and down in the earth." From Daniel 10 we see that his fallen angels apparently have charge of countries, and Dr. Goodwin—an Oxford divine of the seventeenth century—says that the wicked spirits appear to be confined to special places, for when the Lord Jesus cast the legion of demons out of their victim "they besought Him much that He would not send them out of that country" (Mark 5:10, *paraphrase*). Elsewhere in the Scriptures you have traces that they find some relief when they can get access to the bodies of human beings, and that, when they go out of them, they roam restlessly about, wandering up and down in "dry places," seeking rest, and finding no relief until they can again enter the bodies of men.

Christian workers will surely be powerless in reaching men until they recognize that all these forces are at work as "world-rulers of [the] darkness" (Ephesians 6:12, *ASV*) which the world is wrapped in, but the enemy is making so many blind to these facts that they are groping about like blind men, knowing very little of what is going on around them, and even using carnal weapons to try to destroy the kingdom of their spiritual foes.

Here are these forces round about us in the air, holding human beings in their power, under the direction and control of their head and prince, who is called the Deceiver of the whole inhabited earth. There is absolute unity among the satanic forces, *though there is not unity in the church of Jesus Christ*. The forces of evil are all agreed to obey their head and to carry out his will implicitly. When the Lord cast out the legion of wicked spirits from a man, Goodwin points out, how completely agreed were a whole legion to go to the same place, and not to take different ways. The whole legion—actually six thousand—went in one direction, carrying out one purpose. Oh, that we children of God might understand how persistently the enemy works to divide the servants of God! What folly to be busy "working for God" and at the same time blind to the disaster of divided forces against a united foe.

It is striking to read in the book of Judges that "God sent an evil spirit between Abimelech and the men of Shechem" (Judges 9:23), so that "the men of Shechem dealt treacherously with Abimelech"—the end being judgment and death. Here God is spoken of as the Sovereign Power of the universe, by whose *permission* alone the emissaries of Satan are allowed to work. When men sin against Him, or disobey Him, He has simply to withdraw His restraining hand and let the powers of darkness in the air work their will upon them, so as to bring judgment upon them.

Again it is said, *"God sent an evil spirit"* to trouble Saul (1 Samuel 16:14), because Saul would not obey the Lord—*i.e.*, Saul refused to obey God, therefore God permitted the emissary of Satan to have his rightful place, for "rebellion is as the sin of witchcraft," said Samuel. But disobedience or sin is not always the cause of God permitting their attacks, for God permitted Satan to attack Job so as to prove to the principalities and powers in the heavenly realm his integrity and loyalty to God. God set the limit—as He always does—and brought His servant right through to the place of double blessing. Again, God permitted an evil spirit to provoke David to number Israel, but he need not have been deceived if he had listened to the protests of his servant Joab. Here we see that unwillingness to listen with an open mind to others gives place to the enemy and brings on the suffering of judgment.

To Peter again the Lord said, "Satan hath desired to have you, that he may sift you as wheat" (Luke 22:31). Peter had not been disobedient then, but there was in him hidden material of self-confidence which the enemy could use, and unless it was dealt with he would have been unfitted for God's use at Pentecost. Peter was loyal to Christ and unconscious that he would be capable of a fall into oaths and curses, denying the Lord, after those years of fellowship with Him. It is clear, in light of the ground for the enemy thus disclosed, that the blessing of Pentecost would have been a terrible danger to Peter unless the Lord had permitted Satan to attack him to bring it to light. Paul, too, was attacked by "a messenger of Satan"—an evil spirit permitted to "buffet him"—so that he might not become exalted. He was very exalted when he started on his journey to Damascus, and this trait of his natural character evidently needed dealing with to the end of his days. Peter and Paul—both of them apostles of Christ, and yet God permitted Satan to attack them. This is just what God is permitting with many of His children now. "Satan hath desired to have you, that he may sift you as wheat; but I have prayed for thee," said Christ to Peter. The sifting work is done most frequently by attacks of the enemy, upon *ground in us unknown to ourselves*. So it is clear that it is not always specific disobedience, or specific sin, which brings the onslaught of the powers of darkness.

Look again at the case of Paul. He says, "There was given to me a *messenger of Satan* to beat me. I asked God to take it away, and He said, 'No, I will give you grace to conquer.'" What was it given for? "*Lest I should be exalted above measure*, through the greatness of God's working in me!" Thus you see, by this case in point, how God permits the evil spirits—the emissaries of Satan—to attack the servants of God for their development in the strength of God, and their knowledge of His triumphing power.

Reverting again to the realm of the enemy, Goodwin points out how the powers of darkness can send a "breath" over a whole town, or country. By his hosts of wicked spirits Satan can raise a tumult, as he did in Ephesus against Paul. You remember how the crowds "all ran into the theater" shouting, not knowing why they did so (see Acts 19:29–32). It was the enemy that raised the riot against Paul, twisting his words, and seeking to destroy him. Have you noticed how "doctrines of demons" run like the wind, while Christ's truth has to cut its way inch by inch through the darkness in the atmosphere and in the minds of men? This may be why the spirit of error is described as wind—"carried about with every wind of doctrine . . . after the wiles of error" (Ephesians 4:14, *ASV*).

At this present time we are in the stage of the church's history which Paul expressly foretold by the Holy Spirit's command, the closing of the dispensation, when "some shall fall away from the faith, giving heed to *seducing spirits* and doctrines of *demons*" (1 Timothy 4:1, *ASV*). "Oh," said a brother the other day, "I don't understand about evil spirits. I understand about *Satan* tempting." Yes, but since the prince of the power of the air is not omnipresent, like God, *does he not work through emissaries*? He is the mastermind, it is true, and he conceives the "devices" and the plans to frustrate the ripening and maturing of the church; but the attacks and the plans are carried out by the subordinate forces.

It appears just now as if the abyss has been opened (Revelation 9:2) and there are pouring out upon the church these hosts of deceiving spirits, with "doctrines." The special attack of Satan's hosts upon the church in the latter time will be along the line of doctrines or teachings—"wiles of error." They go like wind! You know some of them, and how they "catch on." Why? Because the enemy *holds the air*. It is his realm, and—so to speak—he has a worldwide communication system. He sends out a lie, and it is flashed by evil spirits everywhere, while they cloak and frustrate the making known of the truth—not only the truth of God, but the truth about God's servants who bear the Word of Truth to the world.

Alas! how Satan can dull the minds of God's children, so that they so often believe his lies. You know it in your neighborhood, in your church, in your district. Why does not *God's truth* run through your district as rapidly as Satan's lies? What is the matter? Is there not proof around you? Is it not true in your experience? Is it not absolutely foolish for God's children to be blind on these matters so that they are caught by these "winds" of Satan? They take what is *in the air*—depression, gossip, rumor, lies—and they absorb all into their minds, and, in their turn, act as Satan's transmitters of untruth. Like the Ephesian crowd, they too run and shout, they know not why!

THE ARMOR OF LIGHT

Now let us look at the weapons of victory a little in detail, those making up the "whole armor of God" (Ephesians 6:13–17). Three things you are said to *have* done, and three things you have got to *do* for victory. You *have* braced your mind with truth. You *have* put on the breastplate of righteousness, *i.e.*, you must be living right up to the utmost knowledge of your sense of right and wrong. When you do something that you know is not right, however much you are used to doing it, it is certain defeat before the enemy. And you *have* shod your feet. The Roman soldiers had spikes in their sandals to keep them from slipping.

Then there are three things you have got to *do*—you have to TAKE the shield to quench the fiery darts; TAKE the helmet of salvation to cover your head; TAKE the sword of the Spirit to cut the air. There are days when the enemy gathers around you, and you almost feel difficulty in breathing. Have you ever experienced that? I speak to those who are spiritual. Those who are still "soulish" will not understand what I mean. When your *spirit is pressed down* by forces of darkness, you get a sense of suffocation. This feeling of suffocation affects the body, and makes you feel as though the life was pressed out, until the sense of suffocation is removed. This is the meaning of "burden" in prayer, by which you learn to diagnose spiritual things. You may know by the pressure on your spirit that there is oppression in the air—that the forces of darkness have gathered about the place where God's truth is being preached. Then you resist the "oppression" and, claiming the blood of Calvary, fight through to victory—and there will be victory in the meeting, also, as a result!

These are the prayer-warriors that God wants—who know the spirit-fight, and the way of resistance to the enemy in the air, and victory. We know much about "asking," and about "working"; but you cannot "work" against the powers of darkness. The only way to deal with them is by the attitude of resistance, and prayer. You will know of their gathering around by the oppression in your spirit. You have to know the way to pray out above them. How? By laying hold of the victory of Christ over all the power of the enemy, and using "the sword of the Spirit." That sword will *cut the air*. It is to be used *against the enemy*, not against the people. For instance, you see a soul deceived and misled by the power of the enemy. It is no use arguing with that soul. *He is not in a condition to reason with you*, and you must have eyes to see it. Never reason with a soul that is under the power of the enemy. What must you do? Use the sword of the Spirit to the soul? No, not always; but *always* use it *against the enemy*, use it against the oppression that comes down upon the soul, or upon the meeting. How? The Spirit of God must teach you what sword to use. Sometimes you try many different texts, but none of them seem to cut, until you lay hold of another, and instantly the whole oppression is broken.

"Take the helmet of salvation." What is the helmet for? To protect the head. The main point of attack against the child of God, who is united to Christ in spirit, is the head. Of course, take it while you stand on identification ground! There must be no question about that. "They that are Christ's have crucified

the flesh with the affections and Iusts"
(Galatians 5:24). We are not talking about
that realm, but of the spirit-warfare in the
heavenlies. Here a chief point of attack is the
head. One part of the armor, then, which you
have to *take* and *take continuously*, is the
helmet; something to cover your head. What
is it? The helmet of salvation: *the salvation of
your head as well as your heart*. (See Psalm
140:7.) Is your "head" saved? Is it saved from
your own way of thinking, and its own plans,
and its own ways? Unless your "head" is saved
you need not think of victory here; that is to
say, aggressive victory for the church of
Christ. For here in the heavenlies the body of
Christ is one, and as part of the body of Christ
you are in a general warfare for the whole
church. Remember, the weapon for personal
warfare is Calvary. When you are tempted to
yield to sin, go to Romans 6. Therefore, put on
the helmet.

Many of the Lord's children keep their
minds open for the enemy. They protect their
hearts, but their *minds* are open and un-
guarded. They allow them to lie fallow, to be
open for all that the enemy sends along. They
do not know how to recognize the thoughts
that come to them from evil spirits. Thoughts
of unkindness and criticism and misjudgment
come from evil spirits, and are not your own,
if they do not come from your heart and the
deliberate choice of your will. Evil things that
come into your mind *are not yours* if you

recognize their origin and refuse them.

Beware, too, of a passive mind. If your mind is lying unused, the enemy will gain many a victory. God will quicken your mind, and make it think and reason, and cause you to see what He wants you to do. You need to ask with all your heart, "Lord, make me recognize every thought, word, and suggestion that comes to my mind from Satan's emissaries." Do that, and as quick as you see them, shut the door. *Take* the helmet, and *take* the sword. When the mind is protected by the helmet then you use the sword of the Spirit to cut through the oppression in the air.

Next you need to use the *shield*—TAKE up the shield to quench the fiery darts. Don't try to put the helmet on the head when there are fiery darts *in* the mind already! How many fiery darts have you admitted while you have been in this convention? It is written: *"the fiery darts of the wicked one."* They are forged in hell, and have at the tip a little spark of fire from the pit, which inflames the mind and makes it incapable of receiving the truth. Fiery darts about that friend with whom you are working—a jealous thought so that you are reading in the light of it everything that person is doing. That is what is going on among God's children. Satan has let loose an avalanche of fiery darts among the advancing hosts of God's children, and they have not lifted the shield of faith against them. They have allowed them to enter the mind and burn there. You will often find the mind inflamed with fire that never came from God. You can recognize it whenever you see the face go red and the body get agitated when some special subject is referred to.

Is not this the great truth that the church needs just now: even to take the shield of faith to quench, and to take the helmet of salvation to cover, and to take the sword of the Spirit to cut? This means quiet, deep, steady resistance to the enemy, and a quiet, steady holding of Christ's victory.

In an onslaught by the enemy, have you ever gone to the armory and used this sword against the foe? "The Son of God was manifested to destroy the works of the devil" (see 1 John 3:8). Not *you* manifested to destroy them; *Christ* was manifested to destroy the works of the devil. The battle was fought and won by Him, and what He desires of you is simply that you use *His* victory. "Praying always with all prayer and supplication of the Spirit, at all seasons, and *watching* . . ." (see Ephesians 6:18). Once you understand the conflict, and the forces around you, and the wiles of the enemy to draw you down, you will be always watching. You cannot afford to have slips with your tongue. The devil is taking sentences out of the mouths of God's children today and is using them. He can put a sentence into the mouth of a servant of God now, as he did into the mouth of Peter; and then he sets men to take hold of it and fight over it.

If we will each thus learn to stand in victory, the Lord will bring His church into victory as we are "watching . . . for all saints." The Lamb shall overcome, and they shall overcome who are with Him. Not they who walk in the earthlies and fight for themselves, and similarly fight for the church; but they who walk with *Him* and thus overcome. Listen to Revelation 3:21: "To him that overcometh will I grant to sit with Me in My throne, even as I also overcame and am set down." "There is a place by Me," He says (Exodus 33:21), "and I invite you to a place by Me."

The devil's trick is to keep you down on the earthlies, trying to deal with the *effect* of all you see contrary to God, and not with the cause; he pushes you to try to put things right in the Satan-blinded world and Satan-dulled church with *your own* faculties and strength, instead of understanding that in this spiritual warfare the way of action is union with Christ, "far above all"—there to hold His victory, until we see HIM deliver the souls. If we knew how to do this for the churches, if we knew how to "break through" in the spirit to the heavenly realms, and how to dwell in that place of victory, and see *the Lord* set the souls free, what changes, what progress would speedily be made!

The risen Lord calls you to His throne. He says, "There is a place by Me." I give you that call from Him. May it come to your heart. Will you listen to Him? Part with your place on earth. If you are cast out of your churches, there is a place there. If you are cast out by your friends, there is a place there. Sit there with Him. That is what we need today; that is the place— "there is a place by Me." "I will give to him to sit down with Me . . ." (Revelation 3:21, ASV).

"These shall war against the Lamb, and the Lamb shall overcome them, . . . and they also shall overcome that are with Him . . ." (Revelation 17:14, ASV). But ". . . they are called and chosen and faithful." It depends on our being *faithful.* You must be *faithful.* It is not that you are to be a success; but *faithful.* The Book of Revelation is all about war. War against the two witnesses, when apparently they were overcome, and their bodies were left to lie in the street of the city for three and a half days, while all who dwelt on the earth made merry because they thought they had got rid of them; but the hour came when the witnesses went up into heaven in the sight of their enemies. WAR. There was WAR against the Lamb, and there was WAR against the church. Read and understand, and you will see the way of victory.

If you, children of God, will break through into the heavenly light, God is going to break forth among us in mighty power. God grant it! May the Lord lead us on to victory. Amen.

CHAPTER 3

A GLIMPSE INTO LIFE IN THE SPIRIT

"They that are after the Spirit [mind] the things of the Spirit" (Romans 8:5).

W E NEED to know more of the life and walk "after the Spirit" if we are to live above the things of earth and triumph in the spirit-warfare. The spirit needs liberating so that it may become dominant, and in control of the soul and body. Fausset says that when Adam was created the spirit was dominant, the soul was the vessel through which the spirit acted, and the body was a servant to the soul and spirit; but when Adam fell the spirit sank down into the vessel of the soul, and the soul down into the body—the "flesh"—and he "became flesh." Instead of the spirit ruling the flesh, the flesh dominated the spirit. The Lord said later on, "In their going astray they are flesh" (Genesis 6:3, *footnote ASV*). These words describe men as they now are when unregenerate.

Christians do not understand "spiritual conflict" in the Lord's service because they do not know how to live in the Spirit. Let us consider this spirit-life as it is revealed in the New Testament. I have already referred to the threefold nature of man. Paul writes, "The very God of peace sanctify you wholly . . . spirit and soul and body" (1 Thessalonians 5:23). "Spirit"—that is the inner shrine where God dwells. "Soul"—that is the mental and emotional life, making up the personality. "Body"—that is the outside case, the shell, or the "sheath," as Daniel described it: "I was grieved in the midst of the sheath" (7:15, *Aramaic, footnote ASV*). Your body is not the whole of you; your mind is the vehicle for thinking, but your spirit is to be the active power, and in that spirit the Holy Spirit desires to dwell. This tripartite nature of man is placed in the order of importance by the Apostle Paul in the words "spirit and soul and body."

God begins His work by regenerating the spirit in man. We have a natural human spirit of which God says, "a new spirit will I give you," and then He adds, "I will put My Spirit within you" (Ezekiel 36:26–27). Paul continually refers to his own spirit apart from the Spirit of God. We are born of the Spirit when

God regenerates the human spirit, giving a new spirit. "That which is born of the Spirit is spirit" (John 3:6). Becoming a child of God is not by becoming a member of a church and looking like a Christian; but it is through God giving you a new spirit, so that His Spirit may dwell in you. God said, "I will dwell in them, and walk in them" (2 Corinthians 6:16). "Having then these promises, dearly beloved, let us cleanse ourselves from all filthiness of the flesh *and spirit*" (2 Corinthians 7:1). There is a cleansing of the spirit that God may dwell in us. On the ground of the precious blood of Jesus Christ, God cleanses us from sin.

In his first letter to Corinth, Paul refers to the spirit of man: "What man knoweth the things of a man, save *the spirit of man?*" (2:11). It is the spirit within us which makes us know ourselves—a deeper knowledge than with the mind. This spirit regenerated is joined to the Lord in union, for "he that is joined unto the Lord is one spirit" (1 Corinthians 6:17). The Spirit of Jesus and your spirit—one spirit, so that as He moves in your spirit you move with Him through an essential union of the spirit with Him.

How is this brought about? Let us look at Calvary, and see how much Calvary has to do with it. Calvary is the place where God does His work in us. It is said our Lord was "put to death in the flesh, but made alive in the spirit" (1 Peter 3:18, *ASV*). It is as you enter the fellowship of Christ's death that your spirit is quickened, and brought into resurrection union with Him. Therefore the need of knowing the cross as the very basis of this life after the Spirit. Just as the Lord was put to death on Calvary, and quickened in the spirit, so you must go to Calvary and in spiritual meaning "be put to death in the flesh." The flesh must be accounted crucified (Galatians 5:24) so that the believer may "walk by the Spirit" day by day, and not fulfill the desires of the flesh (Galatians 5:16, 25, *ASV*).

When Jesus our Lord was on Calvary's cross He "poured out His soul unto death" (Isaiah 53:12), but He said to His Father, "Into Thy hands I commend My spirit" (Luke 23:46). His Father took charge of His spirit so that the power of darkness could not touch it. He also sent His angels to watch His body so that Satan could not touch it in its quiet resting place. If he could have taken hold of Jesus' dead body and energized it as a counterfeit Christ, he would have done so; but God put His angels there to guard it while He took charge of the spirit.

We are to be brought into ever-deepening fellowship with Christ's death. The knife must go deeper and deeper into this earth-life until we are severed from all things that tie us to the earth. Your spirit cannot dwell and move and live in God unless you are willing to let the Holy Spirit apply the death of Christ's cross to you, and cut and cut until, as Peter says, you are "judged according to men in the flesh" so that you might "live according to God in the spirit" (1 Peter 4:6).

It costs to let the knife be taken to this earthly life, and until God cuts deeper and deeper none of us knows how intimately linked we are to the things of this world. Oftentimes we have thought we have gone through the deepest fellowship of His death, then God has put us into new circumstances, and we have discovered we were not as deeply severed as we thought. The price we have to pay for this deep union in spirit, and the consequent victory in spirit over the powers of darkness, is great, but we want not only personal victory but a being brought to that place where God can exercise through us that complete mastery over the powers of darkness which the apostles knew. Jesus sent them forth with the commission to cast out evil spirits. They were to be co-workers with Him. At this present time for the deliverance of the whole church of God we must go on to know the full victory in Christ at any cost.

Each time your spirit goes under and faints in the testing and trials which come to you, you lose mastery over the powers of darkness—that is to say, you get below them instead of abiding above them in God. Every time you take the earth standpoint and think as men think, and talk as men talk, and look as men look, you take a place below the powers of darkness. The mastery over them depends upon your spirit abiding in the place

above them, which is the place of knowing
God's outlook, God's view, God's thoughts,
God's ways, God's plans—by abiding with
Christ in God.

You may be so entangled in the things of
earth that your spirit cannot rise above them.
The devil knows this, and pours the earthly
things upon you to keep you down, so that
you go under and not over when the battle
comes.

I recently read in an American paper the
words: "If God is omnipotent, why does He let
the devil go on? Why not stop him? Because
the devil is a most important instrument for
the development of the church." God has not
finished with the devil yet. He is an instrument, by God's permission, for the development of the church. That is to say, if you are
to be overcomers you must have something to
overcome; and everything you overcome is
bound to mean a greater thing to overcome
next time. So if you get victory now you will
have a greater thing tomorrow to get victory
over. In every test you have either to go down
and be crushed, or to go up in spirit-victory;
and that upward move is the overcoming force
of the life of Christ in your spirit. You cannot
live and breathe easily in the earthlies once
you have had that heavenly union with the
Lord, and known the power of the Spirit. You
will never again be able to endure the life
below—you will feel suffocated! This attests
and proves that the new life of God with its

overcoming force has been put into you.

"Being put to death in the flesh"—yes, it must go on and on, for this deep real severing of soul and spirit is not finished at one stroke. Paul says, "I would not have you ignorant, brethren, of our trouble which came to us in Asia: how that we were pressed above measure so that we despaired even of life, but we had the answer that it was death in ourselves that we might not trust in ourselves, but in God that raiseth the dead" (*paraphrase*). So Paul had, in a spiritual sense, to be "put to death in the flesh" continually. All his self-trust had to be kept at a complete end, and he had again and again to be brought to a point beyond his power to endure, where he was compelled to trust in the God that raiseth the dead. (See 2 Corinthians 1:8–9; 13:4.)

You will find the same truth in Romans 7:4. "Ye are dead to the law that ye might be *joined to another*" (*paraphrase*). Death severing for a spirit-union with the Risen One. The one depends upon the other. This is the clothing by the Holy Ghost that God wants you to know. God does not clothe the "flesh" but the *spirit* with that luminous garment of light, which will make you "fair as the moon, clear as the sun, and terrible as an army with banners" (Song of Solomon 6:10) to the hosts of darkness.

The equipping we are needing just now is the clothing of the spirit with the armor of light, so that you will live and move and act and work in the depth of the spirit, from God's view and God's standpoint. The true equipment of the Spirit is a clothing of the human spirit to strengthen it with might by the Spirit of God all the while the believer is being "judged according to men" and kept in utter weakness as to his own power.

The Word of God is the weapon God uses in this work. "The Word of God is living, and active, and sharper than any two-edged sword, and piercing even to the dividing of soul and spirit" (Hebrews 4:12, *ASV*). Calvary deals with the flesh, but the Word of God—the indwelling and inworking Word—divides between soul and spirit. One department of the "soul" is the intellect. There is with many a mixture of intellect and spirit, so that you cannot tell which is which. You cannot discern what God puts in your spirit, nor the difference between what is in your spirit and what is in your mind. How are you to know the difference? Only by experiencing the truth of God's Word, and by God letting it work in you to the dividing of soul and spirit.

You can at least see that it needs to be done, and you can ask for it to be done. If you cannot tell the difference between that which comes into your mind and what is of God in your spirit, ask Him simply to teach you, for the Holy Spirit is the Teacher. God's way is first to show us the need. Do you know that there is a *need* for this division of soul and spirit, so that your spirit may act in purity, without the mixture of the soulish life? Do you see that the Word of God is the knife to do the dividing? There is a dividing necessary, and a dividing that is a "piercing even to the . . . joints and marrow, and quick to discern the thoughts and intents of the heart" (Hebrews 4:12, *ASV*). "Revealing the mental conceptions" is the meaning. "The Word of God is quick . . . dividing between soul and spirit . . . *discerning the mental conceptions*" (Hebrews 4:12, *Fausset*).

It is clear to all of us that we have a great many mental conceptions of God's Word and truth which never came from His Spirit. Conceptions, for instance, of the way God ought to work—hence our inability to discern His working when He works contrary to these mental conceptions. One of the greatest hindrances to the Holy Spirit revealing to us the will of God is our mental conceptions. You may also have a mental conception of the meaning of a verse which prevents the Holy Spirit from showing you the real meaning of it. This division of soul and spirit is intensely necessary. You find difficulty in guidance simply because God is not able to make His guidance clear to you, because of your inability to discern the difference between the things of your mind and the things of your spirit. Thus the need to know the cross—"being put to death in the flesh"—and of letting the Word of God work in us as a sharp two-edged sword, dividing soul and spirit.

We have seen that the Holy Spirit dwells in the spirit—His Spirit in the inward man. Yes, the body is the temple of the Holy Ghost, it is true, but only so far as being a casing around the shrine in which He dwells. This casing—or sheath—may be quickened by the life of Christ. "If the Spirit of Him that raised up Jesus from the dead dwell in you, He that raised Christ Jesus from the dead shall also quicken your mortal bodies by His Spirit that dwelleth in you" (Romans 8:11). You must know this quickening of the body to a very great extent if you are to be able to endure the conflict at the present hour. Your natural strength will go under, so God quickens your mortal body to make you able to endure what no flesh and blood could bear and live.

One of the temptations in the spirit-warfare is, when the body begins to flag, to say, "I must give up," instead of casting yourself upon "the God that raises the dead," who can quicken the mortal body to endure and triumph in and through all things. God is preparing souls today who are learning the fullest meaning of Calvary. Remember this, rest on this, count on this: "His Spirit in the inward man"; i.e., the Holy Spirit is dwelling in your spirit to strengthen you with might in spirit, soul and body, for all the will of God.

In Ephesians 6 we are exhorted to "be strong in the Lord, and in the power of His might," i.e., in the "strength" of His might (ASV). Oh, how we need strength, for often we can hardly hold our ground. We must have strength. How are we to get a strong spirit? Paul tells us in the words: "Strengthened with might by His Spirit in the inner man." It is the Holy Spirit—the very same Spirit that raised Jesus from the dead—that same Holy Spirit is in your spirit to strengthen you with might in the inward man, and then to quicken your mortal body by His Spirit dwelling in you.

Notice again how Paul speaks of the spirit as a distinct entity apart from mind and body. "God is my witness, whom I serve *in my spirit*" (Romans 1:9, *ASV*). "Serve in *newness of the spirit* and not in oldness of the letter" (Romans 7:6, *ASV*). Then again, he wrote to the Corinthians that he was "absent in body, but *present in spirit*" (1 Corinthians 5:3). "Ye being gathered together, *and my spirit*, with the power of our Lord Jesus" (1 Corinthians 5:4, *ASV*). This describes the close spirit-fellowship with God, and with God's children "in the Spirit." "Stand fast in one spirit" (Philippians 1:27). Here is the union that God wants—a union of spirit with spirit among His people, so that they are one in standing against the enemy in the spiritual sphere.

You will always find that among those who are in this plane of the spiritual life there is a marvelous oneness of spirit, even if they live at the ends of the earth. They meet and they know each other though they have never met in the body before. There is perfect union of spirit. "That they may all be one; even as

Thou, Father, art in Me, and I in Thee" (John 17:21, *ASV*). Such is the unity of spirit in God. When he was in one place, Paul wrote, "I had no rest *in my spirit*, because I found not Titus my brother" (2 Corinthians 2:13). He did not say "I had no rest in my heart," nor "in my mind," but "in my *spirit*." Thus you see how Paul lived and moved and worked in the spirit. Again in Romans 8 we read, "They that are after the flesh do mind the things of the flesh; but they that are after the Spirit the things of the Spirit." How much do you live in the soul and not in the spirit? They that live "after the flesh" are those who in their thinking and acting live according to the mind of the flesh; while those who live "after the Spirit" are most concerned about "the things of the Spirit." The life of the Spirit, the joy of the Spirit, the move in the Spirit, the liberty in the Spirit—"They that are after the spirit [do mind] the things of the Spirit. For the mind of the flesh is death; but the mind of the Spirit is life and peace" (vs. 5–6, *ASV*). We have both realms clearly depicted in this passage. The mind controlled by the flesh—the earthly sphere; or by the Spirit—the heavenly sphere.

"Be renewed in the *spirit* of your mind" (Ephesians 4: 23). Your mind should be dominated by your spirit. The mind—or soul—must become a "spiritual mind" instead of a "carnal mind." The mind should be controlled by the spirit, and not by the flesh. There is a fleshly mind and there is a spiritual mind. It is the spiritual mind that is the sober mind, and is open to the thoughts of God. May God teach us what it means to have a renewed mind—a spiritual mind—that is, a mind clarified and dominated by the spirit, and not by the dulling power of the flesh—a mind able to think soberly and clearly the thoughts of God.

Finally, the Apostle Paul writes to the Galatians, "Walk by the Spirit, and ye shall not fulfil the lust of the flesh" (Galatians 5:16, ASV). When you know the Holy Spirit indwelling your spirit and allow Him to rule your whole being, and you walk according to the Spirit, you will then find a complete mastery over the desires of the flesh. You may claim deliverance from this or that habit of the flesh, but unless the spirit is liberated to rule so that you walk "after the Spirit" step by step, you are sure to go back into the old habit, and even if you do not actually give way, you will want to; and that is almost as bad. God wants you to walk at liberty from the dominion of the flesh, and the way is to let the spirit rule so that the body is completely under the rule of the spirit.

How the spirit is moved to mastery over the spiritual hosts of evil we see in the Lord Jesus when He went to the tomb of Lazarus. It is said in a footnote of the ASV, "He was moved with *indignation in the spirit*" (John 11:33, ASV). He went to Lazarus' tomb with indignation against the prince of death, and that indignation in His spirit burst out with mastery over the prince of death when He cried, "Lazarus, come forth." If you know the life in the Spirit, when your spirit is truly freed from the soul-entanglements and joined to the Lord you will understand how Jesus went to that tomb, for it is the same mighty indignation of God the Holy Ghost in your spirit that gives you victory over the powers of darkness. There is something in your spirit, the instant you see the work of the devil, which bursts from you with an indignation not of the flesh, not of the mind, not of the soulish part—but the mastery of the Holy Spirit in your spirit bursts from you with a flash of divine power. You cannot really act in the deliverance of souls without this inner breaking-forth in the spirit, for that is the movement of God within you; and this is only possible when God the Holy Ghost has clothed your spirit with His divine equipment. Then some deep movement in the center of your being will break forth when you see the devil in the way. The greatest power, after all, is not the greatest "influence" but something which is felt in that quiet mastery which says, "This is the work of Satan," and instantly as you perceive it you resist it in your spirit, with the might of God.

This is the life of victory God wants to bring us to, and you can see the reason for the cross, and for "the Word of God, which effectually worketh also in you that believe" (1 Thessalonians 2:13). On the one hand we go back to Calvary as the basis of all God's working in us, and on the other the Word of God is to work in us continually. Will you let that Word work in you to the dividing of soul and spirit?

There is much more also that could be said about the walking "after the Spirit." There is the "meek and quiet spirit" and the learning how not to move unless in co-operation with the Holy Spirit. You can tell directly if you begin to speak from your soul—from your mental powers. Many people can give beautiful Bible Readings, but these are dead unless they are given by the power of the Spirit through your spirit. You may hear the most exquisite addresses, giving the most magnificent views of truth—all true—but dead. Alas, those who speak them do not always know that these are dead and merely mental productions. It is possible for you so to read your Bibles that you pour out a stream of truth which is *dead*, because it comes merely from your mental light. If it comes from your *spirit* through your *mental faculties which have been clarified and renewed*, then it is light and life; but if from your mind only without the stream from your spirit, then it is useless for meeting the deep need of others.

Then lastly, remember you can only really know truth by experience, for theories are dead, however true they may be. You know the meaning of a text by proving it, by living it. You can only understand what has been said this afternoon about the difference between minding the things of the flesh and of the Spirit, by experience. You can only tell what is of the soul* and what is of the spirit by experience, and asking the Holy Spirit to make you quick to discern which is which. May He lead us on into the fullest life "after the spirit" which we may know.

---

*See also *Soul and Spirit: a Glimpse into Bible Psychology* (in relation to sanctification), by the same writer.

CHAPTER 4

THE REVELATION OF THE VICTOR

"I am the first and the last, and the Living one . . . I have the keys . . ." (Revelation 1:17–18, *ASV*).

L ET us turn now to the revelation of the ascended Lord as the Conqueror, and set forth again the personal basis of victory. In the power of the Living Christ upon the throne we can stand victors in the face of all the hosts of darkness. You must never lose sight of the Victor. Never allow yourself to look at the enemy so as to blot out your clear consciousness of the person of the Victor. Read Ephesians 1:17–23, *ASV*—"that the God of our Lord Jesus Christ, the Father of glory, may give unto you a spirit of wisdom, and REVELATION in the KNOWLEDGE OF HIM; having the eyes of your heart enlightened [Gr., *filled with light*]; that ye may know . . . the exceeding greatness of His power to us-ward who believe, according to that WORKING OF THE STRENGTH OF HIS MIGHT which He wrought in Christ when HE RAISED HIM FROM THE DEAD, and MADE HIM TO SIT at His right hand in the heavenly places, far above all rule, and authority, and power, and dominion, and every name that is named . . . and He put all things in subjection under His feet, and gave Him to be Head over all things to the church, which is His body, the fulness of Him that filleth all in all."

Here we have a revelation of the Risen Christ. God raised Him from the dead, and lifted Him right through the plane of the power of the air to the place above "principalities and powers," and made Him to sit at His right hand, with "all things under His feet," and "all authority in heaven and on earth" given unto Him. He is above all rule and authority and dominion and power. He is absolute and complete Conqueror.

In the next chapter the apostle descends from that wondrous unveiling of the Conqueror—which alone the Holy Spirit can give to any heart—to the realm of the earth, and describes the condition of the human race, and the work done for believers in uniting them to the Risen Lord: "You *hath He quickened*." "You . . . who were dead in your trespasses and sins; wherein in time past ye walked according to the course of this world, ACCORDING TO THE PRINCE OF THE POWER OF THE AIR, THE SPIRIT THAT NOW WORKETH IN THE CHILDREN OF DISOBEDIENCE" (Ephesians 2:1–2). It is therefore plainly declared that every soul who is dead in trespasses and sins is walking according to the prince of the air; and that this prince of the power of the air possesses each unregenerate soul, being the "spirit" that now worketh in the children of disobedience. If we take the Word of God as revealing God's viewpoint of all things, we are compelled to see every soul as under the dominion and in the captivity of the power of the prince of darkness—no modifications are given with regard to education or position. If you do not look at unsaved men thus, you will not be of much use to God for their salvation; nor will you trouble much about them; you may even do the very work of the prince of the air by so "christianizing" the exterior of these souls that they will not know the truth about their condition.

Paul comes down from the height of the glorious vision of the Victor of Calvary to this somber picture of the realm of men, and then he rises again, saying (in Ephesians 2:5–6, ASV), "When we were dead . . . made us alive together with Christ . . . and raised us up with Him, and made us to sit with Him in the heavenly places, in Christ Jesus." Can you get a more complete picture of sin, Satan and Christ, and our position toward each, than this? First the Holy Spirit quickened the dead Christ, lifting Him and taking Him to God's right hand—there "made to sit" above all things; then coming down to the poor soul "dead in sin" and under the power of Satan. "And so," Paul says, "because Christ became dead for you, and you are dead with Him, you are quickened with Christ, and raised to new life IN HIM; there is a new life for you."

You are lying *dead* in trespasses and sins. What can you do? Dead people cannot save themselves. And worse than that, you are terribly *alive* in another way. There is a "spirit" working in you, namely, the spirit of the prince of the power of the air. You are not only "dead" to God but you are *active*, and you are active with a satanic spirit to fight against God. You would not be so much trouble if you were only "dead," but you are walking according to the course of this age, which is under the control of the world-rulers—who obey the prince of the air. You cannot save yourself. But the Holy Spirit comes to you, and tells you that Christ died for you—took your place on the cross—so that "through death He might bring to nought" (Hebrews 2:14, *ASV*) the power of the prince of death over you. *Believe* in this atoning sacrifice of the Son of God, even His death for *you*; then there unfolds another life, for He will put into you *new* life—the gift of *eternal* life. By the working of the Spirit of God you are quickened with that life as you accept His death for you, and your death in Him. And just as Christ was raised from the dead into newness of life, you too, joined to Him, will be able to sit with Him in His place of victory over sin and Satan.

Yes, not only are you quickened, but you were raised with Him in His resurrection life, and taken with Him to His ascension place. You were "made to sit with Him." Your God-given place is there—"far above all principality and power." You are to live in the clear air above the powers of darkness, and not in the mists and the darkness of the course of this world.

This is the picture given in the first and second chapter of Paul's letter to the Ephesians, and it is more than a picture—it is a reality. The Spirit of God is leading the church to know it. You say, "It does not look like it—the church is so dead." Yes, but some of God's children are learning to know this, and, as Stockmayer says, every child of God that will by faith "break through" the plane of the enemy to the ascension place in the clear, pure light above is making a way for others to break through after.

You say, "I do not feel that I experience it!" But this is first a faith position, and if you will apprehend it, and take it, the Holy Spirit will teach you how to abide in your position until it becomes a fact in consciousness. So many of God's children are groping about like men without eyes, but there is an illumination for the eyes of their hearts which will

make these heavenly things a reality to them—
so that they live in the reality, and the blessing, and the fullness, and the power, of communion with their ascended Lord.

I have seen many take the message of the
cross—of being crucified with Christ—and
have seen the power of that message working
in them; but I have wondered why so many
never get through to light and liberty. It seems
that they fail to apprehend their position in
the spirit, in union with the Heavenly Christ.
The cross is the *basis* for this position: it is
the negative side of separation from the power
of sin, and the world, and the devil; but we are
only going to get through the dark hours of
the close of this dispensation as we live in the
light of the glory of union with the Ascended
Lord. God the Holy Ghost is preparing His
people for glory, and, like a Great Master-
workman, He is working behind the curtain,
behind the scaffolding. You do not know what
He is doing, but the building is going up.
Throughout the whole world—China, India,
Korea and other places—God the Holy Spirit
is calling out the members of this glorious
body of the Heavenly Christ, who is seated at
God's right hand; and the body is rapidly
forming, and pressing in spirit to faith union
with the Ascended Head.

What we must do now is to get our eyes
off the darkness around us—a darkness
which is deepening on the world—and live in
personal victory up to the very utmost of the

light God has given us. If we could look from the throne of God down upon the world, we should see the Holy Spirit moving here and there, breaking out wherever He can get an outlet.

As the eyes of our heart are illuminated, we shall not be deceived by the surface civilization of today and imagine "the world is getting better." Nor will you be surprised to find, too, that the "Christianity" of today will stone the prophets as much as did the Jews in the days of long ago. Counterfeit Christianity will always turn upon the true, but with the light of the Ascended Lord you can endure the stones. When Stephen was dying, he saw Jesus standing to receive him. The Lord, who was sitting down, rose to receive the spirit of His faithful witness. It is worth being stoned to see the Lord standing to receive you. Never mind the stones. You must have them. There were two kinds of blessings at Pentecost: the blessing of the Holy Spirit in the winning of souls, and the blessing of stones. Are you prepared for either? You want the blessing of winning souls, but let the Master choose for you the honor of the martyr's stones. It may be easier to become a martyr in China, but God has His martyrs in Wales who are being stoned in the civilized fashion of today.

Be not afraid of the persecution and the scoffing, the opposition and the rejection. It is the prince of the air, the spirit that worketh in every disobedient child. By the stones of earth

God is allowing the enemy to drive His children out from the earthly realm, *to live in heaven*. You know that if you can get a prop on earth you will lean on it; so God says, "Let the devil sweep away the props"; and gladly does the enemy use his permission.

Now that we have had the glory side, let us look again to the foundation, and see if we are grounded on the rock of Calvary. This is in Romans 6:3. You cannot have a being "raised from the dead" unless you are *brought to the place of death*. You must fully understand that you cannot share in Christ's resurrection unless you also have a share in the fellowship of His death. Your foundation is in His death— the place where you must be rooted and planted, so that no storm will draw you out.

They say that the oak tree lengthens its roots in storms. If you are like an "oak," then God will give you many storms to root you. The stronger the power of the divine life in you, the more will God put it to the proof; and as He puts it to the test, it strengthens at the roots. You can never know "Ephesians 1" in unbroken, permanent victory, unless you know "Romans 6" as your unbroken, permanent footing. Do you ask what Romans 6 is? Listen to the apostle: "Are ye ignorant?" Yes, we are very ignorant. Ninety-nine parts of the church are ignorant. They think that Romans 6 is only "theology." They have relegated it to the theological bookshelves. That is of the prince of the air. The devil knows what the sixth of Romans means to him, and so he has managed to put around it all the theological quarrelings possible, so as to hide from the church the only way of victory over him. Are *you* ignorant? "All we who were baptized into Christ Jesus were baptized *into His death*" (*ASV*). Do you know what that means? Do you know what it means for the Holy Spirit to take you and put you into the death of Christ, not in theory, not in an outward and visible sign, but in the real "likeness" Paul speaks of in verse 5?

A Greek scholar pointed out to me once about this fifth verse that the word "likeness" in the last clause is not in the original. Correctly it reads: "If we have become united with Him in the likeness of His death, we shall be also . . . of His resurrection." There is no "likeness" in the resurrection, for it is a *real reception of a real life*. We only get a "likeness" of His death—a glimpse, a shadow of it, a little touch of it, but nothing of its awful depth on Calvary. "Baptized into His death!" I would plead with you not to trifle with this message. When you get to the glory you will most bitterly regret having heard these things and then criticized them as "a mere view of truth," or "an address." If you criticize God's truth, you will have to face it. I plead with you that you will at all costs of this earthly life let the Holy Spirit make real to you what *being planted in Christ's death* means. Only thus can you be conformed to the image of Christ.

There is no other way. "Baptized"—to be put out of sight—"into His death"! Who does it? Surely not the soul itself! It is the Holy Spirit who does the work.

The Holy Spirit has two things to do in a believer, just as He did two things with Christ: (1) At Jordan He baptized Him with mighty power for mighty deeds, but—(2) *Jordan was preparation for Calvary.* When the Christ was on the cross there were no mighty deeds to be seen, yet Calvary did more for the world than all the mighty deeds in Galilee. We think too much of the "mighty deeds" and too little of the death-fellowship with the Master. The "mighty deeds" may mean the "greater works," but the death-fellowship means fruit. You might toil all your life and only do so much, even with mighty deeds; but if you are willing to die with Christ, the multiplication of the fruit will be so great that "your seed shall be as the sand of the sea." *There is no limit to the fruit that comes out of death.* There *is* a limit to "work," even as Christ's works were limited to certain places when He was on earth.

"If we have become united with Him in the likeness of His death" (v. 5, *ASV*). Conybeare says the meaning here is "as a graft in a tree." When the graft is put in the tree there is first a cut made, and then after the insertion the two are bound together with cord. Why? So that the life in the tree might go into the graft, and both tree and graft have one life. Blessed be God for this! When God takes the knife to cut you off, and to graft you into Christ's death, so that His life-sap may flow into you, oh, the fruit of life and joy and peace, and longsuffering, and kindness! The fruit comes from Him, through your life. And what do you do? *Abide in His death.*

How wonderful is the truth which follows the grafting verse—"*Knowing* this [*i.e.*, after knowing the being grafted together], that our old man was crucified with Him." This is God's declaration of the meaning of Calvary. By the apostle He declares that when Jesus Christ hung there, bearing in His own body the sins of the world, our "old man"—the first-Adam creation—was crucified with Him. This is God's record of Calvary. Some say, no, it is Paul's record and estimate; but remember that Paul got his gospel from Christ Himself, and not from men (Galatians 1:12). It was Christ who explained His cross to Paul, showing him that when He hung there the old creation hung there, and died with Him.

Here is the secret of victory over sin. It is not *you* cutting off sin. It is you apprehending your place in Christ's death, and CONSENTING TO BE GRAFTED INTO IT, accounting yourself dead to sin, while the Holy Spirit applies the death-loosing and brings into fact the work of deliverance. The Holy Spirit never fails to bear witness to Calvary. The instant you desire, with full purpose of heart, to be delivered from the power of sin, there is no sin of deepest dye that does not fall away from you there, and you are set free. "The death that He died, He died unto sin once: but the life that He liveth, He liveth unto God. Even so reckon ye also yourselves to be dead . . ." (Romans 6:10–11, *ASV*). Your part is to reckon it, even though you do not understand. To reckon not only that you died with Him, but that you are now, at this very moment, "dead to sin" as far as your choice and your will go. Then—"*Let* not sin reign" (v. 12).

This is the only way of victory over Satan, for it is through sin—known or *unknown*— that he holds us, and it is only as we take our stand on the truth declared in the sixth of Romans—when the devil attacks with his temptation to sin, or when you want deliverance from sin—that you can triumphantly say, "On the ground of my death with Christ, I am now dead to that sin, and it shall not reign." Then the Holy Spirit applies the power of Christ's death, breaks the connection with sin, and you lose even the desire for it. Blessed be God, the conquest is by death, "for he that hath died is justified from sin" (v. 7, *ASV*). The gulf of death comes between you and it, yes, even between you and the Tempter, AS YOU ABIDE IN THE DEATH POSITION.

Again, if you want victory over the enemy holding another soul in bondage, before you deal with that person you must make sure you stand on Romans 6, because the only place where the enemy is powerless is on Calvary ground. Hide in the death of the Lord

Jesus, and in the name of Jesus rise today, and "let not sin reign." Take your place. Reckon you are dead to sin. Cast it off. God will tell you what else to do in the way of action. There—at Calvary—as you learn to abide in His death, your vision will get clearer, the film will pass away, and you will begin to see that on the cross our Conquering Savior shook off from Himself principalities and powers, and put them to an open shame for you. As you in spirit then sit with Him in the heavenly places, you will sing the song of Moses and the Lamb, and find that you are becoming "victorious over the beast." You will read the Book of Revelation as never before, and understand that it is a book of war, and a book of overcoming: and you will see how the Risen Christ in Glory has sent the ringing call from heaven to His church. "*Him* that overcometh," He said, "come up, come up—to *him* that overcometh, to him will I give to eat of the tree of life, even though he dwell where Satan's throne is. . . . To *him* that overcometh will I give authority over the nations . . . because thou didst not deny My name. . . . He that overcometh, I will give to him to sit down with Me in My throne, as I also overcame, and sat down." And "He that sitteth on the throne said, Behold, I make all things new. . . . He that overcometh shall inherit these things"—yes, inherit them. Salvation is a gift, but there is an inheritance of victory—a reward: "*Shall inherit!*" "Now is come the salvation, and the power, and the kingdom of our God, and the authority of His Christ: for the accuser of our brethren is cast down. . . . And they overcame him because of the blood of the Lamb, and because of the word of their testimony; and they loved not their life even unto death" (Revelation 4:1; 2:7, 13, 26; 3:8, 21; 21:5, 7; 12:10–11, *ASV*).

"Unto death, unto THE death!" Death is the secret of overcoming through the blood, and the word of your testimony. God grant it to us all! We are going right ahead, and burning the bridges behind us, for we cannot look back. It must be *on* toward the prize! If the Lord will make you a pioneer in your church, and you keep before them the glory of the Risen Christ, and the overcoming of His foe, and the victory of His death, you will break a way through for them, as the Lord Jesus did for you. Follow His steps, and they will follow in yours, too. The Lord number you among those who are leading souls out to Him, for His glory!

CHAPTER 5

OVERCOMING THE ACCUSER

> *"The accuser of our brethren has been
> hurled down—he who, day after day and
> night after night, was wont to accuse them in
> the presence of God. But they have gained the
> victory over him because of the blood of the
> Lamb and of the testimony which they have
> borne, and because they held their lives cheap
> and did not shrink even from death"* (Revela-
> tion 12:10–11, *Weymouth*).

A SPECIAL characteristic of the enemy
standing in the path of the church is that
of an ACCUSER—"the ACCUSER of our brethren
is cast out." His great attempt to defeat you is
by accusing you. He pours on you, morning,
noon and night, a stream of accusation: "You
are wrong; you are out of God's will," etc.
Have you not been conscious of this stream of

persistent accusation which you thought was all from yourself? Not having recognized the source of it, you have let it turn you in upon yourself, until friends have called you morbid, or hypersensitive, or nervous, or "giving way," while others again say it is your make of character. Is not your self-condemnation one of the great hindrances in your life against a bold, fearless service? You cannot do anything happily because of this stream of "self-accusation," as you call it. You cannot "speak," you have nothing to say; you do not know how to pray; *you* are not fit to be a worker; you are this and that and the other. You are thus turned in upon yourself, and round and round yourself you go, thinking it is yourself all the while. It crushes you and takes the smile from your face, for you are always feeling that you are not what you ought to be, that you never reach your ideals. If you could only be like so-and-so, you might be happy; you have been seeking the blessing he has for years; but everybody can get it but you—and thus you go along with a shadow on your face, a weight on your spirit, and always a mocking word whispered to you, "*You* are always wrong; *you* cannot do anything right!"

There are thousands of God's children who are feeble in God's service because of what just appears to be self-depreciation and self-centeredness. Some go to their knees to seek the baptism of the Holy Spirit, or some other experience, to lift them out of what they call "this low-plane life." They think if they can only get some mighty floodtide of blessing, it would take this shadow off them!

And all the time it is a stream from the enemy AS THE ACCUSER pouring into your mind, as pictures to your mental vision, a flood of accusations about yourself, which, if you only *recognized* that they came from HIM, would cease.

Satan carries out this work by means of his wicked spirits, and their speaking to you is like a ceaseless running commentary upon your actions. That exactly describes the speaking of evil spirits—ceaseless whisperings, morning, noon and night. Now reason it out for yourself: it is not you *thinking*, because there is no action of your brain in the matter. You do not really "think" those things. This ceaseless stream of comment is *forced in on you*, in spite of yourself, although you do not want it. That apparently inward, ceaseless "buzz" of something making comments upon you, and your actions, all the day, is directly from evil spirits of Satan. The moment you recognize it, and *name* it, you are on the first step to deliverance. You say, "I thought it was myself, but I never reasoned it out; now I recognize the accusing enemy. I will take no more 'lies' from lying spirits." They have been whispering in your ears, simply to keep you from being happy and praising God; to stop you having a testimony to give, stop you praying, stop you doing any service for God. The lies of the accuser and his emissaries poured in morning, noon and night can be made to cease through the blood of the Lamb, for "they overcame him by the blood."

I am not now speaking about "conscience." There is a distinction between the deep inward conviction of the Holy Spirit in your conscience, saying, "You know you are wrong," and the nagging whisperings of the enemy.

Then these wicked spirits accuse others to you. These accusations do not come from your heart, nor from your *will*. Who but these same evil spirits make ceaseless comments to you upon everybody you meet? And you take them in, and listen to their whispers. It was neither you nor the Holy Spirit who suggested to you that unkind thought about your friend. Then where did the whisper come from? *Wicked spirits*. They are doing this wicked work in the church, and paralyzing God's children with persistent accusations about themselves, and about their fellow-workers in the Mission, and God's people everywhere.

Now what are you to do? First, recognize "him," *i.e.*, Satan working through his evil spirits. Secondly, on the ground of the blood of the Lamb you say to the accuser, "You are conquered." Thirdly, you give the "word of your testimony," and testify to the victory of Christ, and say to the conquered enemy, "I choose to refuse your lies about myself and others." The Bible calls a lie a lie, and you cannot soften the word when you speak of what evil spirits do. They are *liars*. Satan is a liar. Christ said that he is the "father of lies" and "a murderer from the beginning." Every lie he whispers produces a thousand-fold more.

When these things are pouring in on you, do not ignore them; do not pretend they are not there; do not try to go on with your work and shake them off, for they will not go. They are there, and you must deal with them. Just examine them one moment, and see whether they really come from your *will*, and if they do not, give the word of testimony and say, "I refuse, in the name of Jesus Christ, all the lies from lying spirits, about myself, and my fellow-workers, and about the church." And declare too, "I close my ears to their speaking and refuse it."

These are some of the things that explain why the church is so feeble, and why God's children are so powerless. The Holy Spirit is in the spirits of those who have received Him, but they are powerless because they do not know the enemy. They do not recognize him, and do not refuse him, and do not speak to him, and do not say, "Go, in the name of Jesus!"

What are you to do? When you are in this conflict, you cannot have time always to get away and fall to your knees, and when you do get to your knees these accusing spirits do not stop their work, but pour into your mind while you kneel to pray. You may cry to the Lord and say, "O Lord, stop them," but they do not always stop. Christ has *given you the weapon* to use against them. Just say, "Lord Jesus, I stand with Thee against the powers of darkness," and then say to the enemy, "Go, in the name of Jesus." "Resist the devil, and he will flee from you" (James 4:7).

"They overcame him by the blood of the Lamb" (Revelation 12:11). It does not say here that *Jesus* overcame him, but that the believer overcomes on the ground of the blood. It is *you* overcoming. Christ has overcome for you on the cross, but you have now yourself to overcome on the ground of the blood, and use His weapon. *You* are to overcome, and the Risen Lord says, "To him that overcometh will I grant to sit with Me in My throne" (Revelation 3:21).

It means no self-indulgence, no grasping of anything for yourself. It means that it will take the whole force of the divine life in you to stand, and to overcome.

It is war between the saints and Satan, and the ground upon which they fight and conquer is the ground of Calvary—using what Christ did there. Therefore speak directly to the dragon in your path, and say, "You are conquered!" But do it in dependence upon the Lord Jesus, resting upon the victory of His name and of His blood. Say to the accuser, "I stand in Christ against you," and then declare your testimony, "I choose to be Christ's. I choose to declare in Jesus' name *it shall be victory!*"

CHAPTER 6

BELIEVE NOT EVERY SPIRIT

NOTHING is more necessary in the present day than to "prove all things" along the line of spiritual experiences. It is essential to note:

(1) THE POSSIBILITY OF A CHRISTIAN BEING DECEIVED, for the following reasons:

(a) When a man becomes a child of God, by the regenerating power of the Spirit giving him new life as he trusts in the atoning work of Christ, he does not at the same time receive fullness of knowledge, either of God, himself, or the devil.

(b) The mind, which by nature is darkened (Ephesians 4:18), and under a veil created by Satan (2 Corinthians 4:4), is only renewed, and the veil destroyed, up to the extent that the light of *truth* penetrates the mind—whatever the man is able to apprehend.

(c) "Deception" has to do with the *mind,* and means a wrong thought admitted to the mind under the belief that it is truth. A true and faithful Christian is therefore liable to be deceived by the devil in any sphere where he is ignorant. *Assumed* knowledge is as dangerous as ignorance, since it closes the mind to truth.

(d) The thought that God will protect a believer from being deceived by Satan if he is true and faithful is in itself a "deception," because it throws a man off guard, and ignores the fact that there are conditions on the part of the believer which have to be fulfilled for God's working.

(e) Christ would not have warned His disciples, "Take heed . . . be not *deceived,*" if there was no danger of their being deceived, or if God would keep them from deception apart from their "taking heed" because of knowledge of such danger.

(2) The importance of keeping the balance in truth.

Truth has always two sides. We live with the risen Christ in a new realm where Satan has no place, because Christ is all in all, as far as our spiritual *position* goes. Paul shows this in Ephesians 2:6, but in the same epistle he makes the statement of Ephesians 6:12–17, "We wrestle against, etc. . . . ," showing that while our standing and position is "*living with the risen Christ*," in actual fact the forces of darkness will contest our abiding in that position, and will attack by every conceivable means the *outer man*; hence the need of the armor of *truth, uprightness*, etc., while the full force of the will is indicated in the word "take": "TAKE up to the battle," etc. *Christ* is our life (Colossians 3:4), our inspiring force, but "we live," too, as persons responsible to act and draw upon His life. See Galatians 2:20; Philippians 1:19. The two different sides of the truth are sometimes seen one side more acutely than the other, by different believers, and then they are apt to oppose the side they do not see, as "not Scriptural."

(3) THE NECESSITY OF SEEKING POWER TO DISCERN TRUTH.

The powers of darkness are today taking advantage of *misconception* of truth. God's truth stands unshaken but man's *conception* of that truth may cause him to err. Any materializing of spiritual things opens the door to error. See the materializing of John 6 in the Romish church. The truth of the "Real Presence" is spiritual, not in material bread. So with the baptism of the Spirit, the quickening of the mortal body by the life of the indwelling Christ, and even the truth of the indwelling Christ. The materializing of these spiritual facts opens the door to the watchful "teaching spirits" of Satan. The enduement of power for service is real, and the church of Christ today reaps the fruit from those who have known this enduement, but the "fruit that remains" has come from those who retained the use of their faculties—as Finney and others did—and control of their bodies in such an enduement, and not so much from believers with abnormal visions, etc., which, in numbers of cases, in a few brief months have resulted in the breakdown of the recipient.

And again, in regard to Christ indwelling the believer: The spiritual fact of "Greater is He that is in you than he that is in the world," and "Christ liveth in me" as a "living, bright reality," is blessedly true, but no sober Spirit-taught child of God with "spiritual understanding" and knowledge of the Scriptures will say that this is so literally a fact as to eliminate the "self" to such an extent as to make the believer infallible in judgment, action, etc. The *evil* self-life must go to the cross, according to Romans 6:6, but "self" *as denoting a human personality, remains* to be kept in conformity to the death-life of Jesus. There is no exodus of the self-life through the death of Jesus so absolute as to eliminate the personal responsibility of the believer.

The balance of truth between the divine and the human side is so delicate that there seems not one human being on earth who holds it *perfectly* in every aspect of truth.

Turn where we will, we see even the most sober believers over-balancing on some point or other. Some lean to extreme cautiousness, which blinds them to aspects of truth needed to fill out into the ripeness of maturity what they already know. Others with reckless abandonment fall headlong into pitfalls they do not see. The one need everywhere is recognition of the fact that no one believer, whoever he be, is the *sole emporium of all truth*, and no one believer is an infallible guide into all truth. How patient, then, we need to be with others (2 Timothy 2:24), and watchful over ourselves, according to Romans 12:3 and Galatians 6:1.

Particulars of the magazine
The Overcomer may be obtained from:

The Overcomer Literature Trust
9-11 Clothier Road
Brislington, Bristol
Avon, BS4 5RL, England